Haiku Summer
a haiku for every summer *day*

P.J. REED

Lost Tower Publications

first published in 2021
Revised edition published in 2025
by Lost Tower Publications

P.J. Reed asserts her copyright over this collection of her work.
P.J. Reed is identified as the author of this work in accordance
with Section 77 of the Copyright, Designs and Patents Act 1988.

This book is sold subject to the condition that it shall not, by
way of trade or otherwise, be lent, hired out or otherwise
circulated without the publisher's prior consent in any form or
cover than that in which it is published.

ISBN: 9781800498006

Haiku Summer

also by P.J. Reed

HAIKU NATION

The Haiku Seasons Collection

HAIKU YELLOW
HAIKU SUN
HAIKU GOLD
HAIKU ICE

Simply Senryu

PANDEMICA

Haiku Summer

Haiku Summer: The Haiku Seasons Collection

Foreword

Haiku Summer is the second instalment in the *Haiku Seasons* series by award-winning poet P.J. Reed, continuing her lyrical journey through the changing rhythms of the Devon countryside. In this collection, Reed captures the mosaic of summer. From the shifting colours of leaves and flowers to the soft percussion of waves against the shore, these poems embrace the quiet splendour of the season with tenderness and joy.

Summer is a season of warmth and wonder. The land shimmers beneath golden skies; barbeques crackle to life, and the mouthwatering scent of chargrilled food drifts on the breeze. It is a time of alfresco meals in flower-sweet air, laughter shared around firepits, and conversations that linger long into starlit nights.

Summer is the warmth of sun on skin, the ease of a smile, a fleeting brush with paradise.

In traditional Japanese haiku, poems are composed in three lines following a 5-7-5 *mora* pattern. A *mora* is a unit of sound in Japanese, similar to a syllable though not exactly the same. Because morae do not translate directly into English, syllables are used instead.

The westernised haiku follows a similar structure, using seventeen syllables divided into three lines of five, seven, and five. Traditional haiku avoids rhyme and punctuation, often incorporating a contrast or subtle shift in perspective, usually between the first and third lines, creating two distinct yet harmonious parts. Drawing upon nature and the seasons, these poems distil emotion and reflection into a single breath.

Modern English haiku has evolved from these traditional roots but continues to honour the essence of the form: capturing a moment of beauty within three simple lines and seventeen sound units.

Haiku Summer offers one poem for every day of the season. Each haiku can be savoured as a gentle daily ritual, an affirmation, a reflection, or a moment of quiet meditation.

Above all, *Haiku Summer* is a companion to the soul. May it brighten your days and bring you peace as the season unfolds.

A Note

I love writing haiku in the summertime. There is something about the hush beneath the heat, something in the way the days open wide and unhurried, that invites you to pause, breathe, and notice the smallest things. The delicate landing of a bee on a flower. The slow shimmer of leaves stirred by a wandering breeze. The silence that lingers between birdsongs, like the space between heartbeats.

In my garden, summer is alive in a thousand secret ways. By the back door, tall blue sea thistles sway and nod, transformed into a bumblebee hotel buzzing with tiny guests. The air trembles with their hum, and for a moment, the entire world feels enchanted.

The nearby woods, too, become something magical. Sunlight spills through the canopy, breaking into shifting mosaics of lace and shadow on the path beneath your feet. Walking there feels like stepping through a dream you never want to leave.

This book is my scrapbook of summer days in Devon, stitched together one haiku at a time. Each poem is a held breath, a brief moment I wanted to keep and offer to you, a pocket-sized memory of the season you can carry wherever you go. It has taken four summers to complete this collection, and with every poem I wrote, I fell more deeply in love with the quiet, shimmering heart of the season. I hope it brings you the same joy it gave me.

Inside, you'll find one haiku for every day of summer, from 26 June to 22 September, following the astronomical calendar, though the dates drift slightly each year. The haiku are designed to be read one by one, greeting each morning with a single poem, letting it unfold like a tiny daily ritual. Some readers hold them as meditations, others as affirmations, and some simply take them as small moments of beauty to begin or end a day.

Haiku are brief, but they are never empty.

They hold entire worlds inside them. A single haiku can catch a memory before it slips away, hold a season in the palm of your hand, or gather the fleeting hush of a feeling too delicate for ordinary words.

These haiku are shaped by the Devon countryside, yet their spirit reaches back to the traditional Japanese form, which teaches us to look closely, to fall in love with the small and the ordinary, and to find poetry hidden in the quiet corners of everyday life.

Of course, sometimes haiku can get you into trouble…

Once, while on a haiku walk with Rupert, my big rescue dog, we watched raindrops gather and fall from the tip of a pointed leaf, as I tried to capture the exact moment in words.

We stood there for a couple of minutes, when suddenly I sensed movement behind me. We turned around, and I found a police car!

The officer rolled down his window and called out, wanting to know what I was doing. A farmer had reported us for "suspicious behaviour!"

Apparently, standing still in the rain, staring at a single leaf for far too long, can look rather suspect.

I explained I was in fact writing an ancient poetry farm and not plotting to rob the farm. Fortunately, he believed me and let us go.

However, it was a reminder that sometimes, writing poetry can land you in all sorts of interesting predicaments!

Wherever you are, and whenever you find these pages, I hope these little poems give you what summer gave me: a moment of stillness, a breath of wonder, and perhaps even a smile or two!

'If I put it plainly, it feels like Plath wrote a haiku after spending a weekend in Brautigan's head,' A.

'It is a breathtaking collection that perfectly captures the warmth, joy, and nostalgia of summer. Each haiku is a tiny, vivid moment, whether it's the scent of a backyard BBQ, the sound of laughter echoing on a warm evening, or the feeling of sunshine on your skin. The simplicity of the form makes every word shine, evoking a deep sense of place and season. This book is like a little pocket of sunshine, offering a taste of summer no matter the time of year. A must-read for poetry lovers and anyone longing for brighter days!' G.G.

'I absolutely LOVED this book. When you read the haiku, you can actually envision the smells and feelings of summer. You can even see what the author sees. At the end of the book is the history of the haiku. Hey interesting history. You also have a glossary to help you understand what some words mean. I would love to read more P.J. Reed books,' C.P.

'Not just that the summer haiku is an interesting book, it also discussed the history of haiku as it started in Japan. Apart from the unique poems in the book, it stated what hokku is, which is the opening stanza of renga, and she went ahead to discuss in depth lots of historical factors. Sincerely, this is not just summer haiku; this is amazing, and I will

recommend it to anyone that loves poetry and haiku to be precise,' S.A.

'Haiku Summer takes us on a journey of all that is summer. The very essence of summer. Captivating! Intriguing! The smells, the feels, from sunrise to sunset. Magical! Joyful! Peaceful! Read and allow your soul be enhanced by this vibrant season of warmth. Enjoy!' M.

'Lovely little book of haiku! The spacing of each poem is great. I've been using this in my arts class. We take one haiku each week and paint the scene the poet sets. Great fun!' S.J.

'I love all forms of poetry, but there is something about the haiku that is special to me. I love the format and how short they are, but they pack important meanings behind their limited words. Haiku Summer does just that—each poem having a description of different aspects of summertime. It made me envision the warm feeling and airiness that summer provides, the ocean waves and the bright sun. I loved reading it, and I love that it's part of a series (Haiku Seasons) because I can always place myself in the season I'm missing by reading them.' G.M.

'Haiku Summer is a delicate, luminous collection of haiku that captures summer in small, vivid moments the smell of grass, a breeze, the slow drift of daylight everything that feels like peace before the chaos.' A

Haiku Summer: The Haiku Seasons Collection

Haiku Summer: The Haiku Seasons Collection

Day	Haiku	No.
26 June	alone sea watching	21
27 June	crowding clouds clutter	22
28 June	cow parsley shadows	23
29 June	a little cloud spills	24
30 June	dipolar sunshine	25
1 July	floating storms of grey	29
2 July	the scents of summer	30
3 July	gentle white waters	31
4 July	melting midday sun	32
5 July	hidden in the reeds	33
6 July	left limpets linger	34
7 July	airlifted bagel	35
8 July	raindrops are captured	36
9 July	nature's treasures smile	37
10 July	half-blown wishes fly	38
11 July	an early dewfall	39
12 July	soft leaves are bouncing	40
13 July	bird songs after rain	41
14 July	shadows yawn and stretch	42
15 July	cows in the corner	43
16 July	spade stands abandoned	44
17 July	windblown colours fly	45
18 July	sea winds blow softly	46
19 July	sea thistle towers	47
20 July	collared dove couples	48
21 July	blackberry surprise	49
22 July	breeze brushed the birches	50
23 July	intoxicating	51
24 July	fuzzy empty clouds	52
25 July	pinkly smelling rose	53

26 July	shadowy grey leaves	54
27 July	planning permission denied	55
28 July	kissed by distant winds	56
29 July	alyssum breezes	57
30 July	seconds tick slowly	58
31 July	swirls of seagulls	59
1 August	prickling of sharp thorns	63
2 August	hedgehog in my hand	64
3 August	fuchsia red balloons	65
4 August	upon watering	66
5 August	her noble head raised	67
6 August	abandoned feather	68
7 August	a playful sea waves	69
8 August	crinkled leaves crackle	70
9 August	thick and loosely lobed	71
10 August	Salcombe sands, Devon	72
11 August	sand in my teacup	73
12 August	dove on the birdhouse	74
13 August	white-tipped tail twitches	75
14 August	the second cropping	76
15 August	leaf fall fell too soon	77
16 August	Saunton sands sunbathe	78
17August	the sky is blazing	79
18 August	sculptures of the sea	80
19 August	fading summer rose	81
20 August	sleeping quackery	82
21 August	tall thistles sway	83
22 August	buttercup fountains	84
23 August	swaying stalks mark time	85
24 August	pink rippled tulips	86
25 August	seascape tapestry	87
26 August	one hundred green balls	88
27 August	polished holly leaves	89

28 August	rolling waves rumble	90
29 August	ruffled lily pads	91
30 August	shorn fields lie empty	92
31 August	wind swirled puffs of cloud	93
1 September	conker cases crunch	97
2 September	sprinkled in pollen	98
3 September	drying rushes sway	99
4 September	tail feathers rustling	100
5 September	thunder clouds rumble	101
6 September	the drought has broken	102
7 September	fluttering colours	103
8 September	purple hatted thistles	104
9 September	the sky has fallen	105
10 September	wind plucked branches bounce	106
11 September	puffy white cloudling	107
12 September	waking this morning	108
13 September	spike of red berries	109
14 September	butterfly petals	110
15 September	birdsongs are silenced	111
16 September	waiting for the sun	112
17 September	cloud-rinsed grass drip-dries	113
18 September	grey and poisonous	114
19 September	an acorn shower	115
20 September	shadows grow longer	116
21 September	wearing white raincoats	117
22 September	a squall of seagulls	118
Appendix 1	How To Write Haiku	123
Appendix 2	A Brief History of Haiku	127
Appendix 3	Glossary	131

Haiku Summer: The Haiku Seasons Collection

Haiku Summer: The Haiku Seasons Collection

JUNE

Haiku Summer: The Haiku Seasons Collection

26 June

alone sea watching
white waves sweep in and leave a
shiny pebble gift

27 June

crowding clouds clutter
watch in whispers as the sun
falls from fractured sky

28 June

cow parsley shadows
grey flowers sway on the path
in a silent dance

29 June

a little cloud spills
bamboo sways and softly chimes
warm raindrops fall

30 June

dipolar sunshine
lane lies clothed in lace shadows
footsteps in hot and cold

Haiku Summer: The Haiku Seasons Collection

JULY

Haiku Summer: The Haiku Seasons Collection

1 July

floating storms of grey
stolen seedlings gust and fly
dandelion clouds

2 July

the scents of summer
winds carry half-curled petals
mixed with drying hay

3 July

gentle white waters
softly tumble to the shore
shining pebbles bathe

4 July

melting midday sun
faces bob in swimming pools
human hippo's pod

5 July

hidden in the reeds
moorhen stands on lily pad
beeping as I pass

6 July

left limpets linger
crustacean condo cluster
unmerged by the tide

7 July

airlifted bagel
shadows fly across the lawn
gull glides overhead

8 July

raindrops are captured
fall into ponds within ponds
leaf overfills

9 July

nature's treasures smile
hidden by the swaying green
beauty is priceless

10 July

half-blown wishes fly
fill the air with magic dust
sprinkled by the wind

11 July

an early dewfall
daisy wears in diamond shawl
dances with delight

12 July

soft leaves are bouncing
stems sway in flickers of green
swollen raindrops fall

13 July

bird songs after rain
a chorus of happiness
the wood is perfumed

14 July

shadows yawn and stretch
the haying lawn lies hidden
under shades of grey

15 July

cows in the corner
under oak tree umbrella
shadows sleep sideways

16 July

spade stands abandoned
mud splattered and forgotten
laughing seagull's dance

17 July

windblown colours fly
grey shades sway along my path
cow parsley shadows

18 July

sea winds blow softly
caressing bronzing bodies
the sea is sleeping

19 July

sea thistle towers
bees bumble through spikiness
wearing pollen shoes

20 July

collared dove couples
sleep on telegraph perches
urban life stories

21 July

blackberry surprise
petals sleep as berries grow
hidden in the green

22 July

breeze brushed the birches
whisper their words forgotten
somewhere a cloud breaks

23 July

intoxicating
sweet scents of summery fruits
loiter in the air

24 July

fuzzy empty clouds
dandelion skeletons
of wishes half-blown

25 July

pinkly smelling rose
folded like a handkerchief
petals drilled and pressed

26 July

shadowy grey leaves
sail over sun-touched ripples
across river's bed

27 July

planning permission denied
paw prints left on dusty leaves
rabbit trench half dug

28 July

kissed by distant winds
sparkling waves whisper secrets
headland lost in mist

29 July

alyssum breezes
fluttering white butterflies
flower hop and fly

30 July

seconds tick slowly
as the moon falls from the sky
darkness hides away

31 July

swirls of seagulls
glide on wisps of white and grey
waves curl and tumble

Haiku Summer: The Haiku Seasons Collection

AUGUST

Haiku Summer: The Haiku Seasons Collection

1 August

prickling of sharp thorns
a blackberry flavoured wind
berry clusters bounce

2 August

hedgehog in my hand
lying in the dying grass
sniffs honeyed water

3 August

fuchsia red balloons
unresisted temptation
loud pops of delight

4 August

upon watering
sleepy calendula wakes
long lashes flutter

5 August

her noble head raised
little grey doe watches me
I am intruder

6 August

abandoned feather
flutters on the haying grass
memory of doves

7 August

a playful sea waves
and tugs at the drying sand
the shingle dances

8 August

crinkled leaves crackle
hot wind steals cidery breaths
a red apple falls

9 August

thick and loosely lobed
hanging in the oaken leaves
little acorn sits

10 August

Salcombe sands, Devon
paddle boats and sleepy yachts
lounging in the bay

11 August

sand in my teacup
waves jingle their retreat
their laughter hidden

12 August

dove on the birdhouse
disappointed fluttering
an empty seed bowl

13 August

white-tipped tail twitches
sunbathing beneath the oak
little fox and me

14 August

the second cropping
dusty blackberry clusters
burst through nettle banks

15 August

leaf fall fell too soon
green acorns crunch underfoot
the fields are tired

16 August

Saunton sands sunbathe
the rumbling wild waves laugh
seadogs bark and sway

17 August

the sky is blazing
flowers wither on their stems
gardens turn to hay

18 August

sculptures of the sea
waves carve pictures on wet sand
with seaweed and shell

19 August

fading summer rose
petals soft as rabbit ears
float onto the grass

20 August

sleeping quackery
hidden beneath drooping trees
heads tucked under wings

21 August

tall thistles sway
a fluster of leaves and spikes
hungry bees bumble

22 August

buttercup fountains
bees drink from fluted petals
sunlight sprinkled grass

23 August

swaying stalks mark time
dandelion days have passed
wishes have all flown

24 August

pink rippled tulips
gentle petals, cold to touch
milkshake memories

25 August

seascape tapestry
sand dunes and sunken footprints
scattered with white shells

26 August

one hundred green balls
hanging in the olive tree
  a heating garden

27 August

polished holly leaves
pierce the dying hedgerows' shade
thorn points are sharpened

28 August

rolling waves rumble
thunder hidden underneath
white tips on blue waves

29 August

ruffled lily pads
float on the greening river
yellow flowers burst

30 August

shorn fields lie empty
bales stacked like lego towers
stalks crunch underfoot

31 August

wind swirled puffs of cloud
fluttering white butterflies
petals fall and fly

SEPTEMBER

Haiku Summer: The Haiku Seasons Collection

1 September

conker cases crunch
scorching sun lingered too late
a leaf flutter fall

2 September

sprinkled in pollen
bee pauses in his travels
as the blackbirds sing

3 September

drying rushes sway
brown velvet tops explode
in a puff of seeds

4 September

tail feathers rustling
beak cleaning and duck diving
wing washing parties

5 September

thunder clouds rumble
grey-lined shroud covers the sky
raindrops bounce on leaves

6 September

the drought has broken
raindrops fall from bouncing leaves
watched by hidden shrew

7 September

fluttering colours
russet leaves fall from steel skies
grass is painted green

8 September

purple hatted thistles
fluffed seed heads waft in the wind
ready to fly free

9 September

the sky has fallen
silver clouds trapped in puddles
rippling under rain

10 September

wind plucked ranches bounce
base in the leaf harmony
apple at my feet

11 September

puffy white cloudling
watches me through closed window
writing cloud haiku

12 September

waking this morning
the sky wears a silken scarf
a grey raindrop print

13 September

spike of red berries
hidden in the elder shadows
the cuckoo pint trap

14 September

butterfly petals
flap in the misting breezes
sways of cyclamen

15 September

birdsongs are silenced
unbuzzed bees hide in hollows
the first fever falls

16 September

waiting for the sun
green face flutters in yellow
the late sunflower

17 September

cloud-rinsed grass drip-dries
grey skies fill with bulging shapes
the wind feels cooler

18 September

grey and poisonous
mushroom umbrella opens
shelters little mice

19 September

an acorn shower
reflections in a puddle
rain clouds are empty

20 September

shadows grow longer
the sun shared its golden hues
turned and rolled away

21 September

wearing white raincoats
grey clouds sail across the sky
hazel tree shivers

22 September

a squall of seagulls
tap dance after heavy rain
a murder in morse

Haiku Gold

If you would like to continue your daily haiku journey through the changing seasons, step into *Haiku Gold,* a poetic celebration of the golden days of autumn spent in the heart of the Devon countryside.

Each haiku captures a fleeting moment of summer's warmth, inviting you to slow down, notice the world around you, and find quiet joy in nature's smallest treasures.

To explore my full range of poetry books, please visit my website at

And if you enjoyed this book, I would be very grateful if you could leave a review on Amazon.

Thank you so much for reading!

Haiku Summer: The Haiku Seasons Collection

Appendix One

Haiku Summer: The Haiku Seasons Collection

How to Write Haiku

Everyone has his or her own writing style, and it is always important to let your writer's voice come through in your writing. Some forms of poetry are defined by their structure: two-line Urdu love poetry; sonnets, which are fourteen-line poems written in iambic pentameter; and limericks, which use a five-line anapaestic metre and a strict AABBA rhyme scheme.

Writing a traditional haiku is an exercise in bending your words into a concise structure. Many poets liken the art of haiku writing to playing chess: it requires strategy and mathematical precision. As with any skill, haiku needs practice, and with practice you develop a way of thinking that automatically responds to the 5-7-5 syllable scheme that is immediately recognised throughout the world as haiku.

I find my best writing moments are away from people, just walking with my dog or alone and watching nature without the hindrance of man. I have often been asked by the few passers-by what I was doing, as I stood and memorised the mechanics of a droplet of water falling from a leaf. On these occasions, it is always better to reply that you are writing haiku and not, in fact, watching a leaf. One reply will get responses such as 'very noble' and 'how exciting!'. The other will get you a sideways glance and a wide berth.

Once I have observed and the tingling of a haiku begins to form, I try to write down, normally in the first two lines, what I have just seen.

The juxtaposition comes in the final line and will be either a comment on the picture formed, an extension of the image to other areas, the picture from a differing point of view, or even what happened afterwards. So, while the last line is still related to the first, it is obviously different.

However, the most important thing about writing haiku is to have fun and not take it all too seriously!

Appendix Two

Haiku Summer: The Haiku Seasons Collection

A Brief History of Haiku

Haiku is an ancient Japanese art form that traces its origins to the Heian period of Japanese culture (794–1185). During this time, it was considered essential for members of polite society to recognise, recite, and participate in *renga*, a collaborative, long-form poetry composed at social gatherings and lavish house parties.

Renga was one of the most esteemed literary arts in pre-modern Japan. These poems followed sound unit patterns of 5–7–5 and 7–7, typically ending with a series of two-line stanzas in 7–7 rhythm.

Poets of this era prized the use of *utakotoba*, poetic language, as the essence of a perfect *waka* (a classical Japanese poem). The use of more casual or unrefined language was considered unbecoming of true poetry.

Hokku was the opening stanza of a renga poem and held special importance. It was often written by the host or a guest of honour.

H*okku* comprised seventeen morae (sound units), arranged in three phrases of 5, 7, and 5 morae. Unique among the stanzas, it included a *kireji,* or cutting word, placed at the end of one of its three lines. Like all classical Japanese writing, it was written vertically from top to bottom, rather than horizontally as in Western writing.

In the sixteenth century, amid military conflict and the rise of the Tokugawa shogunate, Japanese poetry began to shift. It became more accessible and less ornate.

By the time of the great haiku master Matsuo Bashō (1644–1694), the *hokku* had evolved into an independent poetic form. It appeared on its own or as part of *haibun,* a blend of prose and *hokku*, and *haiga*, a combination of image and *hokku.*

In the late nineteenth century, Masaoka Shiki (1867–1902) formally renamed the standalone h*okku* as haiku.

A traditional haiku contains three lines: the first and last with five *morae*, the middle with seven. A *mora* is a unit of sound in Japanese. It is similar to a syllable in English, though not equivalent. Since *morae* cannot be directly translated, Western adaptations use syllables instead. An English haiku typically follows a 5–7–5 syllable pattern across three lines.

Traditional haiku have no title, no rhyme, and usually no punctuation. However, they often include a *kireji*, a verbal punctuation, and a *kigo*, which is a seasonal reference.

A haiku usually presents a juxtaposition in the first or third line, dividing the poem into contrasting parts. Nature and the seasons are central themes, with thoughts and feelings distilled into a single breath.

Appendix Three

Haiku Summer: The Haiku Seasons Collection

Glossary

Haibun   A combination of prose and haiku.

Haiga   A picture combined with haiku.

Haijin   The writer of haiku.

Haiku   Haiku is a highly structured form of Japanese poetry. In Western culture, haiku is easily recognisable from micro-poetry by its structure. Haiku consists of three lines. The first line contains five syllables, the second seven syllables and the third five syllables. Traditional haiku must contain certain elements, such as a *kigo* and a seasonal element. It consists of a moment in nature captured and recorded.

Haiku Moment   The intense focus on one moment in time. To capture and freeze that image in haiku before it is lost or altered by the passage of time.

Hokku   The original form of haiku. The opening stanza of a *renga.* A long poem written by many people as a form of entertainment for the ruling elite of Japanese society.

Juxtaposition	When sentences are placed together with a contrasting effect.
Kigo	A word that implies the season of the haiku.
Kireji	A cutting word that denotes a break between the two parts of the haiku when writing in one-line Japanese poetry. There is no English equivalent of this, although some poets may put a dash in their haiku to denote the change.
Koan	A *koan* is a Zen Buddhist contemplative phrase that contains a logical contradiction or paradox designed to challenge the reader
Mora	The *mora* is a unit of sound in the Japanese language, which is like a syllable, but not the same.
Sabi	The innate loneliness of life.
Senryu	A form of human haiku, expressing emotions or human actions. It has the same structure as haiku but does not have to contain a cutting word.
Syllable	A syllable is a single sound unit of a word.

Tanka	A t*anka* is similar to haiku but consists of five lines and thirty-one syllables. Each line has a set number of syllables; see below. Line one–five syllables Line two–seven syllables Line three–five syllables Line four–seven syllables Line five–seven syllables
Utamakura	'Pillow Words' used to evoke specific associations.
Wabi	The austere and severe beauty of nature expressed through writings of spiritual solitude.
Waka	Traditional Japanese poetry.

Haiku Summer: The Haiku Seasons Collection

www.ingramcontent.com/pod-product-compliance
Lightning Source LLC
Chambersburg PA
CBHW070915080526
44589CB00013B/1307